THE MIRROR WON'T SMILE UNTIL YOU DO

Jay "King" Sibley

To all those seeking brief respite that nourishes the spirit while flourishing the soul.

The Mirror Won't Smile Until You Do

Written By
Jay "King" Sibley

Front Cover & Photography By
Jarette

Fullcover & Layout By
Sun Child Wind Spirit

Proofread By
Dr. R.R.P.

The Mirror Won't Smile Until You Do

Copyright © 2024, Jay "King" Sibley
All Rights Reserved.

First Edition. Printed In the USA.
Recycled Paper Encouraged.

ISBN-13: 9798344474021

Author Point-of-Contact
Jay "King" Sibley
kingdom_minded01@yahoo.com
Instagram: IAm_JKing1
TicTok: @IAm_JKing1
IAmJayKing.com

Self-Publishing Associate
Dr. Mary M. Jefferson
BePublished.Org - Chicago
(972) 880-8316
www.bepublished.biz
mari@bepublished.org

TABLE OF CONTENT

ᘓᑳ

TABLE OF CONTENTS

Introduction

The Mirror Effect

Every morning, we face a mirror.

We see our reflection staring back at us,

eyes wide open, maybe a little groggy,

and sometimes hesitant. The mirror

shows us who we are, or so we believe.

But what if I told you that the mirror only reflects what you bring to it? That it is more than glass, more than a simple reflection, it is a metaphor for life.

The truth is simple: the mirror will not smile unless you smile first. Your external world is a reflection of your internal state. In this short guide, we are going to explore how you can shift

that internal state, embrace who you

are, and see the world smiling back at

you.

Chapter 1

Smiling From The Inside Out

Happiness is an inside job. We are

the creators of our own experience.

How we see ourselves in the world is

the foundation for how the world

responds to us. If you smile from within, if you cultivate inner peace, gratitude, and self-love, the world will begin to reflect that back to you.

EXERCISES

- **GRATITUDE PRACTICE:** Every morning, write down three things you are grateful for. Keep it simple. Focus on the good in your life.

1._____

_____

2._____

_____

3._____

_____

Examples:

☆ "I am grateful for my life."

☆ "I am grateful for knowing love."

☆ "I am grateful for experiencing joy."

o **AFFIRMATION PRACTICE:** Look into the mirror and say three positive affirmations about yourself each day. Write them down so you don't forget these gems.

1._____

_____

2._____

_____

3._____

_____

Examples:

☆ "I am worthy."

☆ "I am enough."

☆ "I am capable."

Chapter 2

The Power Of Perspective

What we see in the mirror is shaped by our perspective. Two people can look at the same mirror and see completely different things. One might see flaws, while the other sees potential. The difference lies in how they perceive themselves, and that perception colors everything else in their lives.

Perspective is powerful. It has the ability to transform a situation, a relationship, or even a life. The key is learning to see the opportunities hidden within challenges, the lessons

within setbacks, and the beauty in
imperfections.

EXERCISES

o **REFRAMING THOUGHTS:** When you think negatively about a situation, pause and ask, "What is another way to view this?" Write down your original thought and reframe it in a more positive way.

Original:_____

_____

_____

_____

_____

_____

_____

_____

Reframed:_____

_____

_____

_____

_____

_____

_____

Chapter 3

The Mirror Of Relationships

Relationships are powerful mirrors. They reflect back our fears, insecurities, desires, and dreams. How we interact with others often reveals how we feel about ourselves. If you notice a recurring pattern in your relationships, whether it is conflict, misunderstandings, or distance, it is worth looking at what that mirror is showing you.

Our partners, friends, and family members reflect back our inner world. If we feel insecure, we may project that insecurity onto them. If we feel unworthy of love, we may push people away or attract relationships that reinforce that belief.

The first step to improving your relationships is to improve your relationship with yourself. The more you love and accept yourself, the more you will attract loving and supportive people into your life.

EXERCISE

o **RELATIONSHIP REFLECTION:** Think about a challenging relationship. What is it reflecting back to you about yourself? Write down any insights.

_____

_____

_____

_____

_____

Chapter 4

Smiling At Life

Life is a mirror that reflects back what we project into it. If we approach life with fear, negativity, and doubt, those emotions will be reflected back at us in our experiences. But if we approach life with a smile, with hope, gratitude, and openness, we will begin to see those same qualities reflected in the world around us.

The key to a joyful and fulfilling life is not waiting for the mirror to smile first. It is taking the initiative to smile from within, knowing that the mirror will eventually reflect that smile back at you.

Life reflects back what we project into it. Approach life with a smile, and the world will smile back.

EXERCISE

○ **LIFE SMILING PRACTICE:** Smile more throughout the day. Smile at people you pass. Smile when you look in the mirror.

Chapter 5

The Practice Of Self-Love

Self-love is the foundation of a happy and fulfilling life. It is not a selfish act; rather, it is the most important relationship you will ever have. When you love and take care of yourself, you set the standard for how others treat you, and you have more to give to the people and world around you.

Self-love involves accepting yourself as you are while continually striving to become the best version of yourself. It is about nourishing your body, mind, and spirit. This chapter will guide you through practical self-love exercises, including setting boundaries, practicing self-care, and silencing your inner critic.

Self-love is not selfish; it is essential. When you love and take care of yourself, you set the standard for how others treat you.

EXERCISES

- **SELF-CARE RITUALS:** Take time each week for something that brings you joy.

- **LOVING AFFIRMATIONS:** Write down three affirmations reminding you to love yourself. Repeat them daily.

1._____

_____

_____

2._____

_____

_____

3._____

_____

_____

Chapter 6

Chasing Purpose, Not Perfection

Many people fall into the trap of perfectionism, constantly striving for flawlessness and feeling unworthy when they inevitably fall short.

Perfectionism is a losing game, it is rooted in fear, anxiety, and self-judgment.

Instead of chasing perfection, pursue purpose. Find what lights you up, what gives your life meaning, and let that be your guide. When you are focused on living out your purpose, the pressure to be perfect diminishes. You will find joy in the process, even if the outcome is not flawless.

Perfectionism is rooted in fear and self-judgment. Instead of chasing perfection, focus on purpose. When you live out your purpose, the pressure to be perfect diminishes.

EXERCISE

o **PURPOSE DISCOVERY:** Reflect on what makes you feel alive. How can you incorporate it more into your life?

_____

_____

_____

_____

_____

Chapter 7

Embracing The Journey Of Growth

Growth is a lifelong journey. It is not about reaching a final destination but rather continuing to evolve, learn, and expand. Along the way, you will experience highs and lows, triumphs and setbacks, but each step forward brings you closer to your true self.

Embracing the journey of growth means letting go of the need for immediate results. It is about enjoying the process, celebrating small wins, and allowing yourself to be imperfect. The journey is where life happens, do not rush through it, but savor every moment.

Growth is a journey. Along the way, you will experience highs and lows, but each step forward brings you closer to your true self.

EXERCISES

- o **PROGRESS REFLECTION:** At the end of each month, reflect on how far you have come. Write down what you have learned.

Month 1

_____

_____

_____

_____

_____

_____

_____

_____

Month 2

_____

_____

_____

_____

_____

_____

_____

_____

_____

Month 3

_____

_____

_____

_____

_____

_____

_____

_____

Month 4

_____

_____

_____

_____

_____

_____

_____

_____

Month 5

_____

_____

_____

_____

_____

_____

_____

_____

Month 6

Month 7

_____

_____

_____

_____

_____

_____

_____

_____

Month 8

_____

_____

_____

_____

_____

_____

_____

_____

Month 9

_____

_____

_____

_____

_____

_____

_____

_____

Month 10

_____

_____

_____

_____

_____

_____

_____

_____

Month 11

Month 12

_____

_____

_____

_____

_____

_____

_____

_____

Outro

Reflections On Your Journey

As you reflect on the ideas and exercises in this guide, remember that the journey to self-love, inner peace, and fulfillment is ongoing. The mirror will continue to reflect back what you give to it. Each day is a new opportunity to smile first, to approach life with gratitude, and to deepen your relationship with yourself.

Your world will smile back at you, sometimes slowly, sometimes quickly, but the smile always begins with you. Trust the process, be kind to yourself, and keep smiling.

The journey to self-love, peace, and fulfillment is ongoing. Each day is a new opportunity to smile first and deepen your relationship with yourself. Trust the process. Be kind to yourself. And, keep smiling.

Expressions

Dedication

To my oldest son -- Darrius, who continues to inspire me with his strength and heart – and, to my baby boy (AJ) and my baby girl (Lyric-Jai) -- you are the light that guides me, and every step I take is to build a better

world for you.

To my parents, Charles and

Natalie Green, whose love and

resilience shaped me. You taught me to

dream, to believe, and to fight for what

matters.

To my sisters, Krishna and Twyla,

and my brother, Jason -- thank you for

being my roots, my balance, and my

constant reminders of where I come from and who I am.

To everyone who has stood by me, believed in me when I couldn't believe in myself, and supported me even through the toughest days -- your unwavering faith has carried me through storms.

To the person who made this journey possible, whether through encouragement, patience, or love, I owe so much to you.

And to anyone who feels like they're down to their last hard try -- this is for you. When the weight of the world is pressing you down and you feel like you've given all you have, remember that there's always another step forward. This is dedicated to your courage, your persistence, and your spirit. You are not alone.

GRATITUDE

To you, the reader-thank you. This is for you. Your time, your attention, and your willingness to connect with these words mean everything. Whether these words bring you comfort, inspiration, or just a brief escape, know that I am deeply grateful for your presence here.

This work is not only a reflection of my journey but a testament to all of us who continue to move forward, even when the path seems uncertain. So, to you who has taken the time to read this-thank you. Your support, your spirit, and your connection with these pages bring them to life.

THE ART & ARTIST

THE MIRROR WON'T SMILE UNTIL YOU DO by Jay "King" Sibley invites readers on a transformative journey through seven engaging 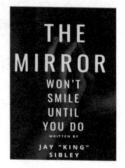 chapters, each designed to spark introspection and inspire action. Sibley expertly weaves personal anecdotes and practical strategies, encouraging individuals to embrace intentionality in their interactions.

Published with the assistance of BePublished.org in October 2024, Sibley's debut literary work challenges readers to reflect on the inner self, suggesting that the world mirrors your own mindset and energy. A universal guide packed with themes of positivity relevant at any stage of life, **THE MIRROR WON'T SMILE UNTIL YOU DO** offers stories of relatable and diverse experiences to help readers spark meaningful conversations that foster connections and cultivate a better life across generations.

With each turn of the page, discover how cultivating positivity and authentic connections can lead to a more fulfilling life. Dive in and unlock the secret to a happier existence! After all, the mirror won't smile until you do!

Available around the world as a Kindle ebook, **THE MIRROR WON'T SMILE UNTIL YOU DO** by Jay "King" Sibley is also available internationally as a paperback / softcover book from online and bricks-and-mortar book retailers including your favorite bookstore.

THE AUTHOR

Jay "King" Sibley was born in Texas,

the third of four children. He has been immersed in singing and the creative arts from a young age. Inspired by watching his mother sing, Jay's love for music blossomed at the age of four and has remained a constant throughout his life.

Though music has

always been his first passion, he also has a deep love for reading and songwriting. Now, after years of creativity and expression through music, Jay has decided to embark on a new journey-writing a book  while also continuing to work as a Master Barber, singer and model.

IAmJayKing.com

Made in the USA
Columbia, SC
10 November 2024

45225751R10041